GLEN HANS

Didn't He Ramble

 Alfred

Produced by
Alfred Music
P.O. Box 10003
Van Nuys, CA 91410-0003
alfred.com

Transcribed by Dan Begelman.

Printed in USA.

ISBN-10: 1-4706-3187-3
ISBN-13: 978-1-4706-3187-1

All photos by Danny Clinch
Design & Layout by David Cleary & Glen Hansard

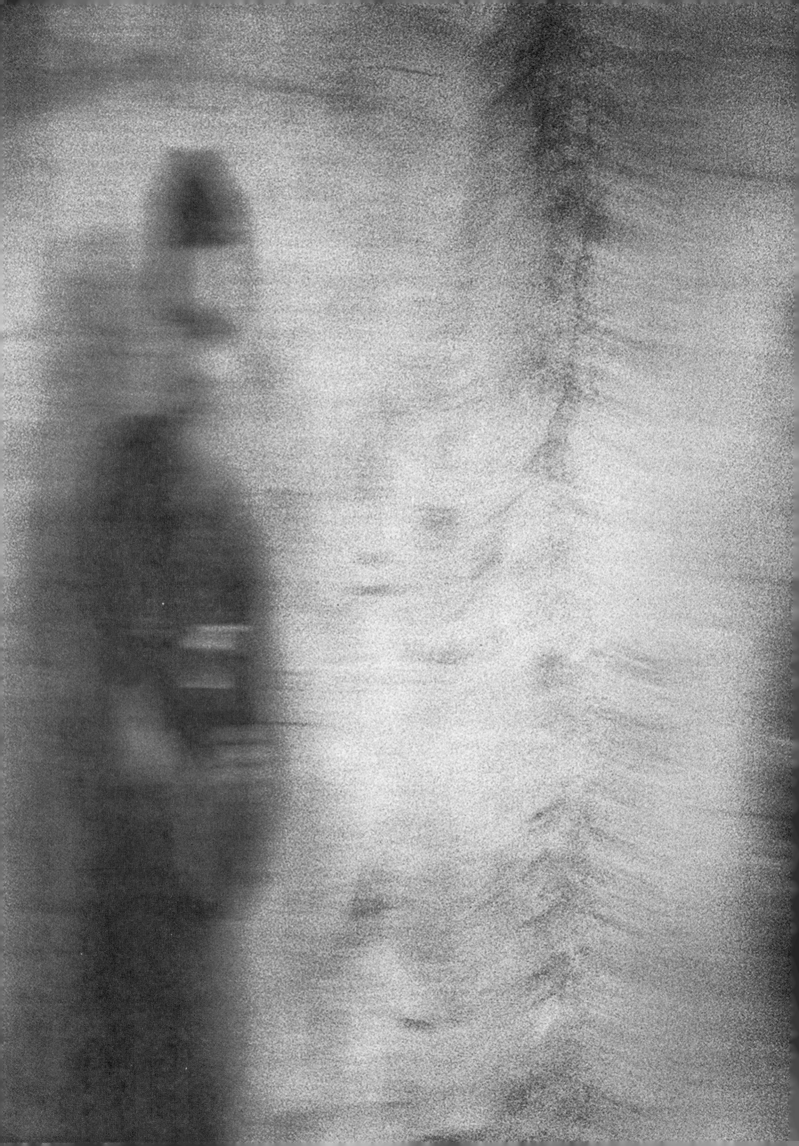

Contents

Grace Beneath the Pines

There'll be no more running round for me,
no more backing down, you'll see —
whatever lies in store for me,
I'll get through it.

There'll be no more going half the way,
you'd better listen to these words I say —
whatever ties they bound to me,
I'll cut through them.

Now I found some
Grace beneath the judge's gavel,
Grace among my brothers on the firing line,
Grace upon this road less travelled,
Grace beneath the pines, the pines,
Grace beneath the pines.

There'll be no more running round for me,
no more going down, you'll see —
the line is drawn; my enemy
better stay behind it.

There'll be no more lifting half the weight,
my will is strong, my back is straight —
whatever lies they told to me,
I'll see through them.

Now I found some
Grace beneath the judge's gavel,
Grace among my brothers on the firing line,
Grace upon this road less travelled,
Grace beneath the pines, the pines,
Grace beneath the pines.

There'll be no more running round for me,
no more going down, you'll see —
I'll get through this.

Words and Music by GLEN HANSARD
© 2015 PLATEAU RECORDS LIMITED
All Rights Administered by WB MUSIC CORP.
Exclusive Worldwide Print Rights Administered by ALFRED MUSIC
All Rights Reserved

Wedding Ring

Where you running to now, baby?
Running all the time.
Where you running to now, darlin'?
Running to all the time.
Well, I sure hope it's to your sister
and not that mean brother of mine.

I've been trying to reach you, darlin'.
I try, I try in vain.
I've been trying to reach you, darlin'.
Though I try, I try in vain.
I always end up losing you
and walking home in the rain.

Wedding ring, wedding ring;
little band of gold.
Wedding ring, wedding ring;
little band of gold.
Will you be strong enough to keep her,
keep her love from going cold?

There's a wildcat in you, woman,
a wildcat on the prowl.
There's a wildcat in you, woman,
a wildcat on the prowl.
Everytime I put my arms around you
I can hear that wildcat growl.

I remember when I met you
there was something about the moon.
I remember the night I met you
there was something about the moon.
I don't know if it was waxing or waning,
but I knew that you'd be leaving soon.

Wedding ring, wedding ring;
little band of gold.
Wedding ring, wedding ring;
little band of gold.
Will you be strong enough to keep her,
to keep her love from getting old?

Words and Music by GLEN HANSARD
© 2015 PLATEAU RECORDS LIMITED
All Rights Administered by WB MUSIC CORP.
Exclusive Worldwide Print Rights Administered by ALFRED MUSIC
All Rights Reserved

Winning Streak

Through summers long and winters cold
may you always have someone good to hold,
and may good fortune wait on every bend,
and may your winning streak,
may it never end.

So, roll the dice, boy, 'cause my money's on you,
take my advice now and put your money down too,
because there's something in the eye you can't pretend,
and may your winning streak,
may it never end.

And may the sign
of the Southern Cross
be some comfort to you when you're lost,
and may the devil's evil eye
pass you by.

Well, it's not for glory, I tell you true,
that I do these things I do for you,
but for a promise I made now I must defend,
and may your winning streak,
may it never end.

And may the sign of the cross
be some comfort when you're lost,
help you when you're all broke down,
may the spirit of good brethren
turn you around.

And may the devil's evil eye
pass you right by,
don't you look back my friend,
and may the sisters of good charity
take you in.

Through summers long and winters cold
may you always have someone good to hold,
and may good fortune wait on every bend,
and may your winning streak,
may it never end.

Words and Music by GLEN HANSARD
© 2015 PLATEAU RECORDS LIMITED
All Rights Administered by WB MUSIC CORP.
Exclusive Worldwide Print Rights Administered by ALFRED MUSIC
All Rights Reserved

Her Mercy

When you're kneeling through the hours,
and you're doubting your given powers,
and when you're ready for her mercy,
and you're worthy,
it will come.

When you're sneaking 'round the back door,
and she's waiting for you no more,
and when you're ready for her mercy,
and you're worthy,
it will come.

When the birds are just tuning up still,
and the dawn breaks on your windowsill,
and when you're ready for her mercy,
and you're worthy,
it will come.

It will come
when you're broken,
when your heart is finally open,
when you're down,
down and troubled,
when you're lost among the rubble.

Well, there's sugar on the old spoon,
let's do that two-step around your front room,
and when you're ready for her mercy,
and you're worthy,
it will come.

Mercy, mercy, coming to you,
feel her beauty flowing through you —
she will unbind you, set the word free.
Mercy, mercy.

Mercy, mercy, coming to you,
feel her beauty flowing through you —

Words and Music by GLEN HANSARD
© 2015 PLATEAU RECORDS LIMITED
All Rights Administered by WB MUSIC CORP.
Exclusive Worldwide Print Rights Administered by ALFRED MUSIC
All Rights Reserved

McCormack's Wall

Well, I've not been honest, darlin',
no, I've not been straight at all.
Well, I beg your pardon;
the night we jumped McCormack's wall
I was so happy just to be with you
I'd've said anything at all.
Now I could scream your name
till you do the same,
but I know you won't respond.

Well, here we are.
What can we do?
La din da...
I'm gonna ride black river.

With the lark in the morning
and the dew upon the dawn,
well, a-home we came a-crawling
with our sickness and our song
for all guitar makers;
for the prisoners and the law;
and the fine wine drinkers
who drank their bellies raw;
and to all the good samaritans,
whoever found us in the dark;
and to all who've been
or come between
the lovers in the park;
and to all the Ó Díomasaigh singers
with their roots in holy ground.
And forgiveness still lingers
in the bells above the town.

Well, here we are.
What's there to do?
La din la...
I'm gonna ride on black river.

Lowly Deserter

Lowly deserter, sing that old song,
and sing a new one for the men
still in battle, far from heaven;
raise your voice up and sing to them.

Lowly, lowly, it must be lonesome,
take a hard look at yourself,
and your brother still in battle;
sing his praises, or don't sing again.

When that question comes to find you,
don't deny you never ran,
and when that feeling comes to take you,
take you walking the streets of hell.

When that question comes to find you,
don't deny you never ran,
and when that feeling comes to take you,
take you walking the streets of hell.

Words and Music by GLEN HANSARD
© 2015 PLATEAU RECORDS LIMITED
All Rights Administered by WB MUSIC CORP.
Exclusive Worldwide Print Rights Administered by ALFRED MUSIC
All Rights Reserved

Paying My Way

Well, you can't just get what you want
without a little work a day.
And you can't just stick out your hand,
no, it doesn't work that way.

It's gonna be a long one,
I'll be working all night long.
It's gonna be a long one,
but I'm paying my way.

And there's not much joy in the work
unless you're born to do it, they say.
And we gotta get down in the dirt now
if we wanna see some change.

It's gonna be a long one,
I'll be working all night long.
It's gonna be a long one,
but I'm paying my way.

And the heart is sliding backwards
on this long dark night of the soul,
and you're the only thing
that keeps me going on.

It's gonna be a long one,
I'll be working my fingers to the bone.
It's gonna be a long one,
but I'm paying my way.

Well, there's not much change in the weather
on this long walk home to you in the rain.
And there's not much left in the purse now
by the time the bills are paid.

It's gonna be a long one,
I can't wait for that weekend to roll along.
It's gonna be a long one,
but I'm paying my way.

It's gonna be a long one,
I'm gonna take you out dancing all night long.
It's gonna be a long one,
but I'm paying my way

Fair work for fair pay.
Yeah, I'm paying my way.

My Little Ruin

Come on, my little ruin, won't you open up and let us in?
Time has not been kind, but you're still standing here.
Leave a light on in your window, won't you let me see a sign?
It's gonna take more than smoke and mirrors now for me this time.

Come on, my little sorrow, won't you sing yourself a different song?
The melody that made you is now a worn-out sing-along.
Everybody's looking at you, but I can't stand to watch;
I've seen this scene come and go too much.

And oh, how you struggle through the hours
with your sorrow leading the way,
and as you stood there among the cowards,
you were letting them win.

No, I'm not, 'cause you're better than they are,
and I can't say it enough.

That's enough, what are you doing?

Come on, my little ruin, won't you build yourself back up again?
Won't you take the time you were given; you promised it to yourself.
You could stand among the best of them if you could hold your own,
but no-one's gonna do it for you now, but you and you alone.

And oh, how you struggle with your power,
and keep your back tight to the wall,
and as you were counted among the cowards,
they didn't see you at all.

Now you're caught on a rising wave, and I can't get you off,
but I'm not gonna stand aside and watch them tear you up.

No, I'm not,
'cause you're better than they are,
you're better than they are,
you're better than they are,
you're better than they are,
and I can't say it enough.

Words and Music by GLEN HANSARD
© 2015 PLATEAU RECORDS LIMITED
All Rights Administered by WB MUSIC CORP.
Exclusive Worldwide Print Rights Administered by ALFRED MUSIC
All Rights Reserved

Just to Be the One

I will understand you,
I will serve you well.
I'll suffer when you leave me,
            stand out in parallel.
And I will recognise you
    when you're lost to yourself,
                just to be the one
        you call in.

I will raise an army,
I will gather strength.
I'll follow where you lead me,
        I'll go through anything.
And I will heed your warning,
    and sound your victory bell,
                just to be the one
        you call in.

And for the first time
        you were dark,
caught out on a western swell,
                    swept apart.
And we watched as their
                bodies danced
            towards the rocks,
    to the rocks.

I will recognise you
when you're lost to yourself,
                just to be the one
        you call in.
            Just to be the one
        you call in.

Words and Music by GLEN HANSARD
© 2015 PLATEAU RECORDS LIMITED
All Rights Administered by WB MUSIC CORP.
Exclusive Worldwide Print Rights Administered by ALFRED MUSIC
All Rights Reserved

Stay the Road

Tired, tired eyes look up and see
all you've done, the path you've come,
the things that you've achieved.
And when you're doubting
I hope you'll trust in me.
Tired, tired eyes look up and see.

I've been mining down a dark hole,
I've been mining in the rocks
for a golden seam she's got buried deep
somewhere inside of her.
I've been working for your wonder,
I've been mining hard and long,
and I will not fold; I'm gonna find that gold,
now my work has just begun.

Come on, pilgrim, won't you stay the road?
Put that distance from your mind,
don't you let it show.
Well, it's just a ride, and I'm at your side
if you didn't know.
Come on, pilgrim, won't you stay the road?

I've been mining down a dark hole,
I've been mining in the rocks
for a heart of gold that can't be bought or sold
she's got there inside of her.
I've been working for your wonder,
I've been mining hard and long,
and I won't give up; I'm gonna fill my cup,
now my work has just begun.

Shelter, shelter bell ring out for all below,
keep your doorway open wide,
give us somewhere to go.
And when we're full of doubt,
and we don't know what about,
don't you tell us no.
Shelter, shelter bell ring out for all below.

GRACE BENEATH THE PINES

Slow ♩ = 64
Freely

Words and Music by
GLEN HANSARD

*Chords are implied throughout.

Verse 1:

There'll be no more run-ning 'round for me,__ no more__ back-ing down,_ you'll see. What-ev-er lies__ in store for me,__ I'll get through.__ it.__ There'll be no more go-ing half__ the way, bet-ter lis-ten to this__ thing__ I say. What-ev-er ties__ they bound to me, I'll cut through__ them. Now, I found some

Chorus:

grace be-neath the judg-e's gav-el, grace a-mong my bro-thers on the fir-ing line. Grace up-on this road less trav-eled, grace be-neath_ the_ pines, the pines,__ grace be-neath___ the__ pines.

Verse 2:

Chorus:

WEDDING RING

Moderately ♩ = 104

Words and Music by
GLEN HANSARD

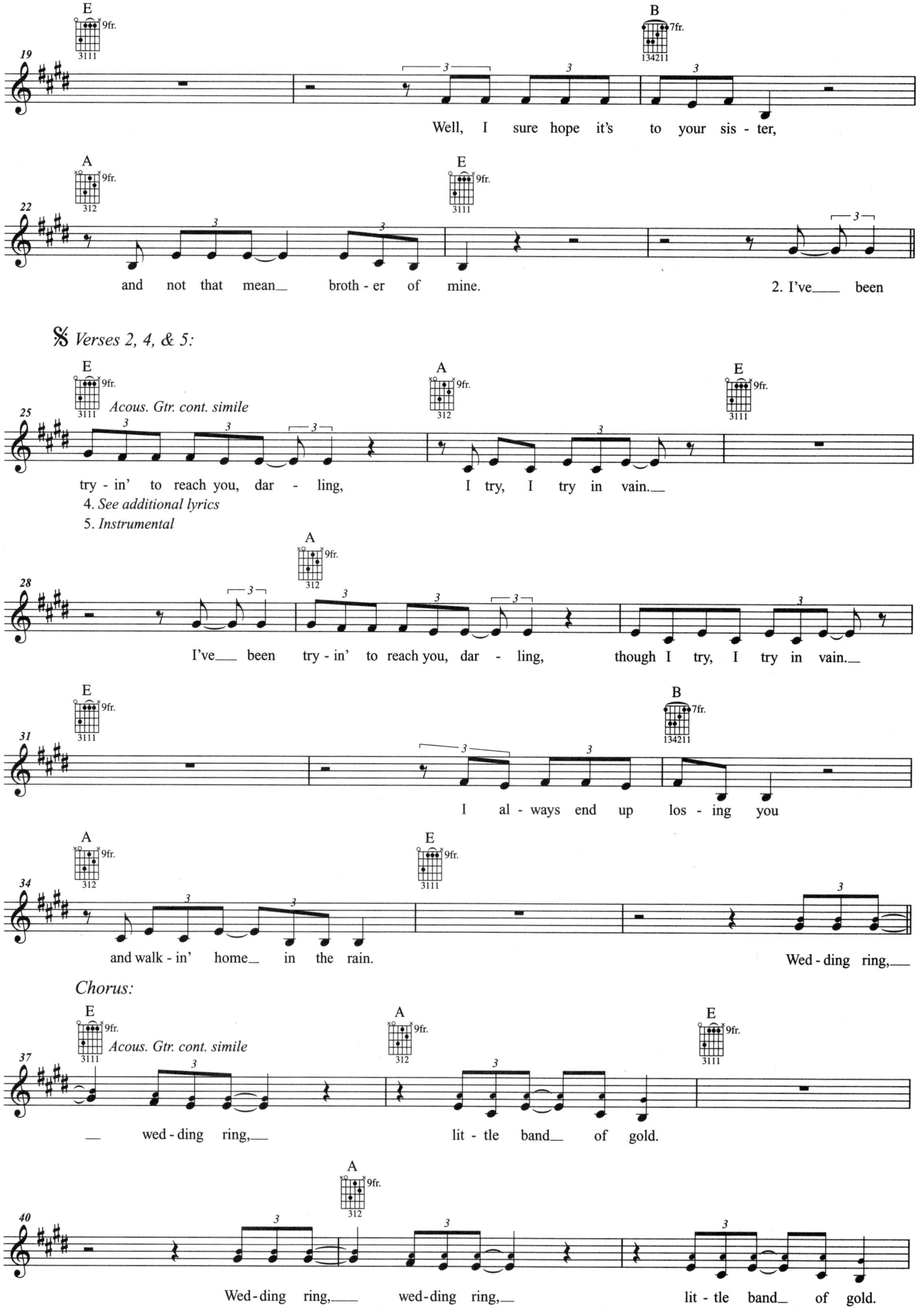
E
B
Well, I sure hope it's to your sis - ter,
A
E
and not that mean_ broth - er of mine.
2. I've_ been
Verses 2, 4, & 5:
E
A
E
Acous. Gtr. cont. simile
try - in' to reach you, dar - ling, I try, I try in vain._
4. See additional lyrics
5. Instrumental
A
I've_ been try - in' to reach you, dar - ling, though I try, I try in vain._
E
B
I al - ways end up los - ing you
A
E
and walk - in' home_ in the rain.
Wed - ding ring,_
Chorus:
E
A
E
Acous. Gtr. cont. simile
_ wed - ding ring,_ lit - tle band_ of gold.
A
Wed - ding ring,_ wed - ding ring,_ lit - tle band_ of gold.

Verse 3:
There's a wildcat in you, woman,
A wildcat on the prowl.
There's a wildcat in you, woman,
A wildcat on the prowl.
Everytime I put my arms around you,
I can hear that wildcat growl.

Verse 4:
I remember when I met you,
There was something about the moon.
I remember the night I met you,
There was something about the moon.
I don't know if it was waxing or waning,
But I knew you'd be leaving soon.
(To Chorus:)

WINNING STREAK

Moderately ♩ = 88

Words and Music by
GLEN HANSARD

Verse 3:
Well, it's not for glory, I tell you true,
That I do these things that I do for you.
But for a promise I made, now, I must defend,
And may your winning streak, may it never end.
(To Verse 4:)

HER MERCY

Her Mercy - 3 - 1

26

Verse 2:
When you're sneaking 'round the back door,
And she's waiting for you no more,
And when you're ready for her mercy,
And you're worthy, it will come.

Verse 3:
When the birds are just tuning up still,
And the dawn breaks on your windowsill,
And when you're ready for her mercy,
And you're worthy, it will come.
(To Bridge:)

Her Mercy - 3 - 3

McCORMACK'S WALL

Words and Music by
GLEN HANSARD

LOWLY DESERTER

Words and Music by
GLEN HANSARD

*Song is performed on mandolin. Chords are arranged for guitar.

PAYING MY WAY

Words and Music by
GLEN HANSARD

Paying My Way - 3 - 2

36

Verse 2:
And there's not much joy in the work
Unless you're born to do it, they say.
And we gotta get down in the dirt, now,
If we wanna see some change.
(To Chorus:)

Verse 3:
Well, there's not much change in the weather
On this long walk home to you in the rain.
And there's not much left in the purse, now,
By the time the bills are paid.
(To Chorus:)

MY LITTLE RUIN

Words and Music by
GLEN HANSARD

Moderately ♩. = 52

Intro:

Do do do do do do._____

1. Come

𝄋 *Verses 1, 2, & 3:*

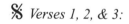

on, my lit - tle ru - in, won't you o -pen up and let us in?

2.3. *See additional lyrics*

Time has not been kind and___ you're still___ stand - ing___ here.

Leave a light

My Little Ruin - 4 - 1

My Little Ruin - 4 - 3

Verse 2:
Come on, my little sorrow, won't you sing yourself a different song?
The melody that made you is now a worn-out sing-along.
Everybody's looking at you, but I can't stand to watch;
I've seen this scene come and go too much.
(To Bridge:)

Verse 3:
Come on, my little ruin, won't you build yourself back up again?
Won't you take the time you were given; you promised it to yourself.
You could stand among the best of them if you could hold your own,
But no-one's gonna do it for you now, but you and you alone.
(To Bridge:)

JUST TO BE THE ONE

Words and Music by
GLEN HANSARD

1. I will un-der-stand you,   I will serve you well.   I'll
2. I will raise an ar-my,   I will gath-er strength.   I'll

*Acous. Gtr. tacet meas. 9–22 (chords are implied).

Just to Be the One - 3 - 1

STAY THE ROAD

*Acous Gtr. in Open D tuning:
⑥ = D ③ = F♯
⑤ = A ② = A
④ = D ① = D

Words and Music by
GLEN HANSARD

Moderately slow ♩ = 76

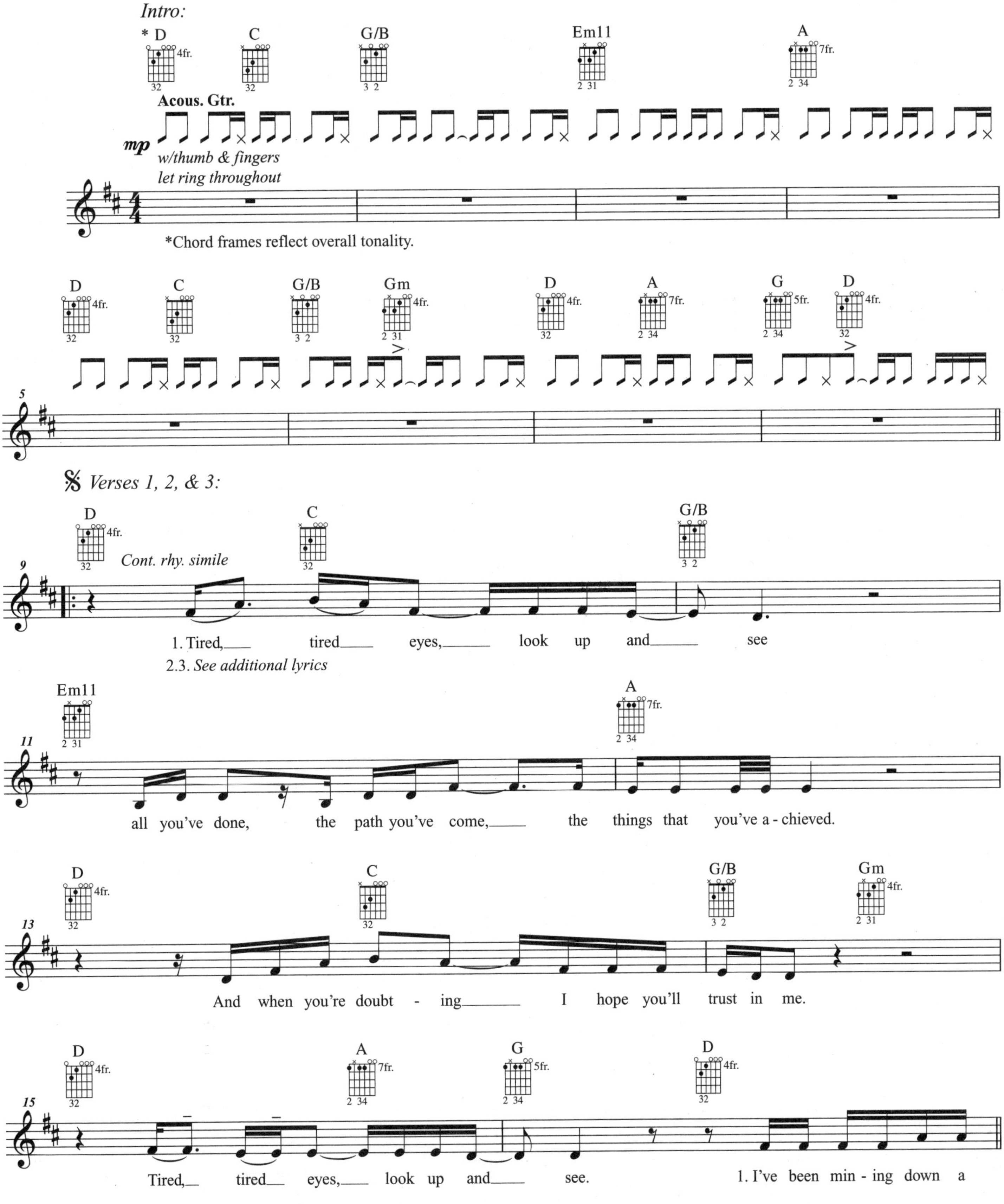

Intro:
*D C G/B Em11 A
Acous. Gtr.
mp
w/thumb & fingers
let ring throughout
*Chord frames reflect overall tonality.
D C G/B Gm D A G D
Verses 1, 2, & 3:
D C G/B
Cont. rhy. simile
1. Tired, tired eyes, look up and see
2.3. See additional lyrics
Em11 A
all you've done, the path you've come, the things that you've a - chieved.
D C G/B Gm
And when you're doubt - ing I hope you'll trust in me.
D A G D
Tired, tired eyes, look up and see. 1. I've been min - ing down a

And when you're doubt - ing_____ I hope you'll trust in me.

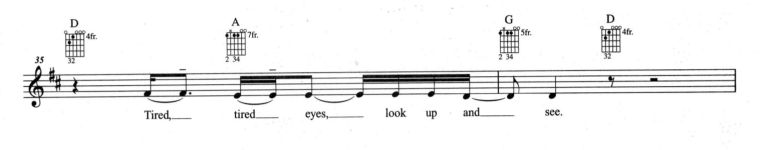

Tired,_____ tired_____ eyes,_____ look up and_____ see.

Acous. Gtr.

Tired,_____ tired_____ eyes,_____ look up and_____ see.

Verse 2:
Come on, pilgrim, won't you stay the road?
Put that distance from your mind,
Don't you let it show.
Well, it's just a ride, and I'm at your side
If you didn't know.
Come on, pilgrim, won't you stay the road?

Bridges 2 & 3:
I've been mining down a dark hole,
I've been mining in the rocks
For a heart of gold that can't be bought or sold
She's got there inside of her.
I've been working for your wonder,
I've been mining hard and long,
And I won't give up; I'm gonna fill my cup,
Now my work has just begun.
(To Verse 4 on repeat:)

Verse 3:
Shelter, shelter bell ring out for all below,
Keep your doorway open wide,
Give us somewhere to go.
And when we're full of doubt,
And we don't know what about,
Don't you tell us no.
Shelter, shelter bell ring out for all below.
(To Bridge 3:)

TABLATURE EXPLANATION

TAB illustrates the six strings of the guitar.
Notes and chords are indicated by the placement of fret numbers on each string.

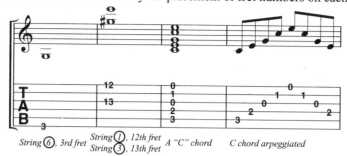

String ⑥, 3rd fret   String ①, 12th fret   A "C" chord   C chord arpeggiated
               String ③, 13th fret

GUITAR TAB GLOSSARY

BENDING NOTES

Half Step:
Play the note and bend string one half step (one fret).

Whole Step:
Play the note and bend string one whole step (two frets).

Slight Bend/ Quarter-Tone Bend:
Play the note and bend string sharp.

Prebend and Release:
Play the already-bent string, then immediately drop it down to the fretted note.

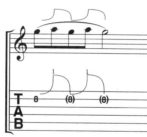

Bend and Release:
Play the note and bend to the next pitch, then release to the original note. Only the first note is attacked.

PICK DIRECTION

Downstrokes and Upstrokes:
The downstroke is indicated with this symbol (⊓) and the upstroke is indicated with this (∨).

ARTICULATIONS

Hammer On:
Play the lower note, then "hammer" your finger to the higher note. Only the first note is plucked.

Pull Off:
Play the higher note with your first finger already in position on the lower note. Pull your finger off the first note with a strong downward motion that plucks the string—sounding the lower note.

Palm Mute:
The notes are muted (muffled) by placing the palm of the pick hand lightly on the strings, just in front of the bridge.

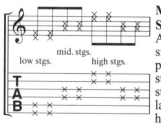

Muted Strings:
A percussive sound is produced by striking the strings while laying the fret hand across them.

Legato Slide:
Play the first note and, keeping pressure applied on the string, slide up to the second note. The diagonal line shows that it is a slide and not a hammer-on or a pull-off.

HARMONICS

Natural Harmonic:
A finger of the fret hand lightly touches the string at the note indicated in the TAB and is plucked by the pick producing a bell-like sound called a harmonic.

RHYTHM SLASHES

Strum Marks/ Rhythm Slashes:
Strum with the indicated rhythm pattern. Strum marks can be located above the staff or within the staff.

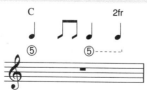

Single Notes with Rhythm Slashes:
Sometimes single notes are incorporated into a strum pattern. The circled number below is the string and the fret number is above.

Artificial Harmonic:
Fret the note at the first TAB number, lightly touch the string at the fret indicated in parens (usually 12 frets higher than the fretted note), then pluck the string with an available finger or your pick.